# Nocturnal Creatures
## Coloring Book

### Ruth Soffer

DOVER PUBLICATIONS, INC.
Mineola, New York

*Bibliographical Note*

*Nocturnal Creatures Coloring Book* is a new work, first published by Dover Publications, Inc., in 1998.

DOVER *Pictorial Archive* SERIES

*International Standard Book Number: 0-486-40362-9*

Manufactured in the United States of America
Dover Publications, Inc., 31 East 2nd Street, Mineola, N.Y. 11501

# Introduction

While most people and many animals are sleeping, a broad range of nocturnal creatures are active in every part of the world. In fact, more varieties of land animals sleep by day and move about at night than do the opposite. *Nocturnal Creatures Coloring Book* introduces 45 varieties of "night workers" from North America, Central America, South America, Africa, Asia, Europe, Australia, and New Zealand. The creatures portrayed include mammals, birds, reptiles, amphibians, and insects. Some are rare, others are common. A few, like the kiwi and the lesser panda, are known worldwide for their unique features. Others, such as the Western native cat and the Malaysian pangolin, are scarcely known beyond their home territories. Some, such as the coyote, porcupine, and raccoon, are familiar to most people who live in North America, but others—like the southern flying squirrel, which also is common in the United States—rarely are seen. The sun bear and the fennec fox are the smallest of their kind. The night monkey is the only nocturnal monkey. The boa constrictor, the ocelot, and the scorpion are feared by many. Most of these nocturnal creatures, in their own ways, are beautiful.

Unlike human beings, who may, for various reasons, choose as individuals to sleep by day and work at night, nocturnal animals are members of species that have evolved, in the course of millions of years, to be active at night. This may have occurred because animals in those species had an advantage in surviving and reproducing if they were active at night, thus avoiding daytime predators. Also, it may have happened because species members that hunted at night were more successful, catching their prey asleep. Some nocturnal creatures live in very hot climates, and emerge only at night, when the sun's rays do not reach them and the air is cooler. Many of these animals that hunt or forage by night are aided by unusually large eyes and ears, or by an acute sense of smell. Most of them are color blind, and also cannot perceive red light, which is why red lightbulbs are used in exhibits of nocturnal creatures in captivity. The animals are active when people are watching them, because it seems dark to them, so they believe it is night.

Several of these nocturnal species are endangered, because much of their habitat has been destroyed. Others have been poisoned by pesticides and pollutants, or they have been slaughtered for their fur or other salable features. Still others have been hunted because they are believed to kill farm animals, or because people fear them for other reasons that may have little or no basis in reality.

*Nocturnal Creatures Coloring Book* gives intriguing glimpses into the lives of many animals that cannot be seen in nature without traveling to several distant parts of the world. Many of the creatures shown in its pages are rarely viewed, even in zoos.

# Index of Common Names

**Scorpions** of the *Centruroides* species live in Florida and other states that border the Gulf of Mexico, and as far west as Arizona, as well as in Mexico. They spend the day underground or beneath stones. At night, they prey on insects and spiders, which they grasp in their claws and paralyze with their tail-sting. They consume their meal by injecting digestive juices into the creature they have captured and sucking the body dry. *Centruroides* scorpions have several pairs of eyes (some along their sides). Female scorpions of these species carry their eggs in a sac and transport the hatched young on their back until they can get around on their own.

1

The **Texas banded gecko** (*Coleonyx brevis*) lives in desert areas in the southern parts of the states of New Mexico and Texas and in northeast Mexico. Its skin is pink-toned, with dark-brown mottled markings. Its protruding white-rimmed eyelids give it a sleepy look. During nightly prowls, these geckos stalk insects and small spiders, twitching their tails in a way that reminds some people of cats. However, the squeak they emit when alarmed is more like that of a mouse. The Texas banded gecko sheds its skin and then eats it. Female geckos are larger than males. They produce two eggs after mating.

The **striped skunk** (*Mephitis mephitis*) is easily recognized by the white stripe up the middle of its forehead, and the white patch at the nape of its neck, which often extends on the black fur to the base of the animal's bushy tail (sometimes white-tipped). Skunks hunt from nightfall to dawn. They eat mice, birds' eggs, insects, berries, and dead animals that they find. When annoyed, a skunk lifts its tail and sprays or squirts a stinging, foul-smelling liquid at the offender, from special scent glands. Skunks do not hibernate; they forage, on relatively warm nights, even in cold seasons. Female skunks usually give birth to five or six young, sometimes as many as ten. Newborn skunks are blind. When they first start to walk, they follow their mother in single file.

The **green lacewing** (*Chrysopa* species) lives throughout North America, in meadows and gardens and at the edges of forests. It is pale yellow to pale green in color, with clear wings showing a network of green veins. The **California green lacewing** is bred indoors and released in greenhouses and vineyards, where it consumes mealybugs—voracious pests that destroy ornamental and food plants, including grapevines. Lacewings lay their eggs on slender white silk stalks, which hang from the undersides of leaves.

The beautiful **luna moth** *(Actias luna)* has pale-green wings with purple borders on the leading edges of the fore wings; the hind wings have long tails. This moth is found only in North America and is an endangered species because so many have been killed by pollution and pesticides. It lives in the broadleaf forests of the eastern United States and southern Canada, where the trees shed their leaves in the autumn. Two groups of luna moths are born each year. The caterpillars develop in a cocoon that usually lies on the ground. Once out of the cocoon, they feed on leaves of hickory, walnut, sweet gum, persimmon, birch, and other trees.

The **Western native cat** (*Dasyurus geoffroii*) is one of five marsupial species (not actually related to cats) found in Australia. They mainly forage on the ground, but can climb well. They are predators that hunt at night, but they eat plant matter as well as insects, mice, and sometimes poultry. Their fur is gray, olive-brown, or dark reddish-brown, with white spots on the back, sides, and heads. The face is paler gray, and the part of the tail nearer the tip is black. Females produce four to six young at a time; they take about two years to reach their full size. The Western native cat prefers open grassland, but now survives only in a few remote areas. Predators, epidemics, and destruction of its natural habitat have severely reduced its numbers.

The **sun bear** *(Ursus malayanus),* native to Malaysia, is the world's smallest bear. It lives in dense forests, usually sleeping and sunbathing in a tree during the day. It does not hibernate. The sun bear's short fur is black, but the muzzle is gray or orange and often there is a white or orange mark on the chest. These shy, very intelligent bears have large paws and strong claws. They eat jungle birds, small rodents, and fruit, as well as insects including termites, and bees and their honey. Females usually give birth to one or two young. One sun bear lived nearly 25 years in captivity.

The **ringtail**, often called the **ringtail cat** (*Bassariscus astutus*), lives in North America, as far north as Oregon, as far east as Kansas, and as far south as southern Mexico. Its banded, tapering, bushy tail often is longer than its body, which has buff-colored fur above, tinged with black or dark brown, and white fur tinged with buff color below. The eyes are ringed with black or dark brown. Ringtails usually make their dens near water, in rock crevices, hollow trees, or abandoned dwellings. They are agile and climb well. Their night hunts are usually solitary and in a regular territory. They capture insects, rodents, and birds, and also eat fruit.

8

The **brown kiwi** (*Apteryx australis*) lives in the forests and brushlands of both the North and the South Island of New Zealand. It is the most common of three species of kiwi (small, flightless birds) that evolved in New Zealand. Its long, yellow bill has a sensitive tip. Nostrils near the tip enable the kiwi to smell underground worms when it feeds at night. This bird has small eyes and poor vision, but its sense of smell is unusually acute. The weight of an egg laid by a female kiwi is about a third of the bird's body weight. This makes kiwi eggs the heaviest known, in proportion to the bird's weight. Their 80-day incubation period is among the longest known; only the eggs of the royal albatross have been known to take one day longer than that to hatch.

The **lesser bush baby** *(Galago demidovii)* is the small-est species of galagos or bush babies, which live in Africa. A forest dweller, living in areas from Senegal to Tanzania, it has dense, relatively long, slightly wavy fur, **rather** like a plush animal made for children to cuddle. Its tail, which has sparser hair, is longer than its body. The lesser bush baby lives in trees, making its nest of leaves or among thick vegetation. Usually each animal sleeps alone, during the day, but sometimes two or three females nest together with their young. Lesser bush babies can make long horizontal leaps between branch-es. They feed on insects, especially small beetles and night-flying moths, and also eat some fruits and tree gums.

The **Malaysian pangolin** or **scaly anteater** (*Manis javanica*), native to Malaysia and Indonesia in Southeast Asia, has a long, tapered body, with overlapping scales on the upper surfaces of the body, head, tail, and limbs. The scales range from dark brown to yellowish; exposed skin on the belly, throat, and other scaleless areas is gray with some blue or pink tinges. Pangolins have small eyes, a short snout, and no teeth. Their long, sticky tongues, which lick up ants and termites, have long muscular roots. Their foreclaws break open ant and termite mounds. Timid creatures, pangolins usually defend themselves by curling up to protect their soft parts within a casing of sharp-edged scales. Young pangolins (usually one is born at a time) ride on their mother's back or tail.

The gentle, curious **lesser panda** *(Ailurus fulgens)* lives in mountain forests and bamboo thickets in Nepal, Sikkim (a state in India), northern Burma, and south-central China. It has long, soft fur, ranging from rust-colored to deep chestnut on the body, with faint rings on the tail. The face fur is mainly white, with dark eye patches. Lesser pandas don't mind cold temperatures.

They usually sleep in a tree during the day. Their diet, besides bamboo shoots, includes other grasses, roots, fruit, and acorns, as well as some insects, eggs, young birds, and small rodents. Females usually give birth to one or two young, who stay with the mother, or with both parents, until the next year's litter is about to be born. Pandas often live in pairs or small groups.

The **night monkey** *(Aotus trivirgatus),* which is called the *douroucouli* in Peru, lives in forests in the northern part of South America. It is the only monkey known to be active at night. Its head and body are more than a foot long, and its furry, nonprehensile tail is about 50 percent longer. The night monkey has good night vision and moves through the trees like an acrobat, running along branches and leaping. Its large, yellow-brown eyes stand out in its black face. The fur is gray-brown on the upper parts and whitish or reddish on the underparts of its body. The night monkey eats insects, lizards, and fruit, and also consumes sleeping birds.

The **tarsier** *(Tarsius spectrum)*, a primate, lives in forests and scrub land on various islands off the coast of southeast Asia. Its hair ranges in color from buff to dark brown on the upper parts of the body, and may be buff or gray below. Tarsiers' big eyes are prominent in their round heads. They can rotate their heads almost 360 degrees (nearly a full circle), which gives them a large range of vision, and their almost hairless ears seem to be always in motion. During the day, tarsiers sleep while clinging to vertical tree trunks or branches. They are able to leap long distances. Rounded pads on their long fingers and toes give them a good grip on any surface they grasp. Tarsiers mainly eat insects. They leap at them and grab them with both hands.

The **collared peccary** *(Tayassu tajacu)* is found in the states of Arizona and Texas, and as far south in the Americas as northern Argentina. This animal's fur usually is dark gray, with a white collar on the neck. The peccary's Spanish name, *javelina,* means javelin or spear and refers to the shape of its upper canine teeth. Collared peccaries live in various areas, from desert scrub lands to forests, in groups of as many as 25. They are active mainly at night and in the cooler hours of the day. They have poor vision, but an acute sense of smell. They like to stay near water. Using their snouts, they collect food on and in the ground, such as cactus fruit, berries, tubers, bulbs, roots, insect grubs, snakes, and small animals. They fight fiercely when attacked.

15

The **nine-banded armadillo** (*Dasypus novemcinctus*) is a small mammal with hard "armor plating" on its body, its tail, and the top of its head. It lives in burrows and rock outcroppings in woodlands and brushy areas, in the southeastern United States from Florida to Texas, and as far north as Missouri, as well as in northern Mexico. Insects are its main food. Armadillos have only vestigial teeth, like pegs. Female armadillos always give birth to four young at a time; those born at the same time are all female or all male.

The **American spadefoot toad** *(Scaphiopus intermontanus)* is related to the European spadefoot, which is found in Europe and the part of Asia called the Middle East. Spadefoots were named because the projection on the side of each of their hind feet, which they use to dig their burrows, was thought to resemble a spade. These toads usually are three to four inches long, and have a soft, moist skin—more like that of frogs than that of most toads. Spadefoots spend the day in their burrows, which they dig themselves into backwards. Many American spadefoot toads live in the dry southwestern part of the United States, especially in areas with sandy soils.

The **aardwolf** *(Proteles cristatus)* has yellow-gray hair on its body, with black stripes. Its bushy tail has a black tip, and its legs are black below the knees. It lives on sandy plains and in bush country, making its dens in holes in the ground. It moves slowly, not covering much territory as it forages at night for termites and insect larvae. Perhaps because of their scraggly appearance, aardwolfs have a bad reputation among farmers for eating chickens, but it seems to be undeserved. Aardwolfs do not hunt live animals or eat dead ones they encounter, and do not seem interested in eating meat at all. If attacked by dogs they can defend themselves with their sharp canine teeth. Female aardwolfs give birth to two to four young at a time.

The **porcupine** *(Erethizon dorsatum)* is dark in appearance, almost black, but its hairs are yellow toward the tips. This creature is known for the long, sharp spines or quills set into its body, which are especially numerous on the rump and the tail. Porcupines, common in the western United States and in Canada, make their dens in hollow trees, in caves, and in rock crevices. They usual-ly live in woods, often stripping off the bark near the tops of trees to eat the bark's inner layers. They also eat buds, twigs, nuts, and berries, and like to lick salt. This short-legged animal walks clumsily on the ground, but climbs and swims well. Its eyes glow brightly white when they reflect any light shone on them at night.

The **garden dormouse** *(Eliomys quercinus)* is native to Europe and has relatives in North Africa and the Middle East. It has short hair, except for most of the length of the tail. The body hair is gray or brown above and cream-colored or white underneath. Usually there are some black markings on the face, and the tail may have three bands of color: cinnamon brown, black, and white. Despite its name, the garden dormouse lives in forests, as well as in swamps, rocky areas, and farmlands. It moves agilely in trees. Its diet consists of acorns, nuts, fruit, insects, small rodents, and young birds. It is considered a noisy animal, and makes a variety of sounds. Two to seven garden dormice are born at a time.

The **spiny anteater** or **short-nosed echidna** *(Tachyglossus aculeatus)* lives in Australia and in nearby New Guinea, which is also home to long-nosed echidnas. It has a domed back, a small head with small eyes at the snout's base, and a stubby tail. Its furry body has long, hollow spines, which may be yellow-and-black or entirely yellow. It runs quickly and climbs well. When threatened, it forms a ball, with its head, feet, and hands protected by the spines. Spiny anteaters live in burrows, hollow trees, and rock crevices. They dig out their chief food, termites and ants, with their claws. They have long, sticky tongues, but no teeth. These unusual animals (monotremes) produce eggs (females incubate a single egg in a body pouch), but newborns suck milk from the mother's mammary glands, as mammals do.

The **silky anteater** *(Cyclopes didactylus)* lives in southern Mexico, Central America, and northern South America. Its prehensile tail may be as long as its body and has no hair on its underside. The animal's soft, silky hair ranges in color from buff-gray to golden yellow, but a line of dark hair runs along its back. Silky anteaters live in tropical forests and are active most of the night, resting by day in shade near treetops. They rarely descend from the trees, where they lick up ants, termites, and other insects with a long, sticky tongue, but they can walk on the ground on the sides of their feet, to avoid standing on the two long, curved, sharp claws on each forepaw. Their hair resembles the fiber in the pods of silk-cotton trees, which they favor as dwellings.

The **genet** (*Genetta* species) is found in various parts of Africa, where ten different species inhabit forests and grasslands. One of those species also lives in three European countries, and in Asia at the eastern end of the Mediterranean Sea and on the Arabian Peninsula. Its soft, thick hair usually is gray or yellow, with brown or black spots of various sizes in rows along its sides, a line of dark hair along the spine, and dark bands on the tail. Genets spend the day sheltered in a burrow, a hollow tree, or a rock crevice, or on a tree branch. At night they stalk birds, rodents, small reptiles, and insects. Females give birth twice a year, usually to two or three young.

23

The **margay** *(Felis wiedii)* resembles the ocelot (see the next page), but it is smaller and more slender, its tail is longer in relation to its body, and it spends more time in trees, where it moves with great agility and hunts effectively. The margay's habitat has been the tropical forests of southern Mexico, Central America, and northern South America, but the animal has been rare and listed as endangered for forty years. Despite the already threatened status of this species, thousands of margay skins and some live animals were still being imported into the United States in 1970, and the numbers of these feline hunters living free declined greatly in later years.

The **ocelot** (*Felis pardalis*) ranges from northeastern Mexico to Brazil. By the early 1980s only a few individuals were left in the United States, near the Texas–Mexico border. A huge trade in ocelots, dead (their skins were sold) and alive (they were sold as pets) endangered the species. Ocelots have dark streaks and spots on fur that is whitish, tawny yellow, reddish gray, or gray. Each cheek shows two black streaks, and the tail has either dark rings, or dark bars on the upper surface. This feline hunts small mammals, birds, snakes, and fish. It climbs and swims well. Ocelots live in both wet tropical forests and dry areas of scrub vegetation.

The Old World **fruit bat,** found in tropical and subtropical regions of Africa, Asia, Australia, and some Pacific islands, has 42 genera and 170 species. Those known as flying foxes *(Pteropus* species*)* are found on many islands off Southeast Asia, and in some mainland areas. Thailand is home to two species, *Pteropus lylei* (seen here) and *P. vampyrus. P. lylei* has large eyes and acute vision. These bats live in very large colonies, which can devastate a fruit crop overnight. They nourish themselves with fruit juices, spitting out the pulp and seeds. After several night hours of feeding and digesting at fruit trees, they return to their roosting areas.

The **California leafnose bat** (*Macrotus californicus*), shown at the lower left, eats moths, which it finds by listening to the echoes of high-pitched sounds it emits. Some moth species have ultrasonic detection abilities that enable them to take evasive action when a bat is approaching. The **lesser longnose bat** (*Leptonycteris sanborni*), shown at the upper right, drinks nectar from the flowers of the saguaro cactus, which open at night, usually for one night only. The plants are pollinated by the nectar-feeding bats, which consume some pollen while spreading it to other flowers. Agave plants also attract these bats. Nectar-feeding bats have long, tubular tongues, which they extend into the deep, narrow flowers to sip the nectar, which consists of sugars and water.

The **slender loris** *(Loris tardigradus)* is found only in southern India and on the nearby island of Sri Lanka. This small, thick-furred creature has large, round eyes, thin, round ears, and no tail. Its fur may be yellowish gray or dark brown on the upper parts of the body, and silvery gray or buff on the lower parts. It lives in mountain forests and other broadleaf forests, sleeping on a tree branch dur-ing the day. The slender loris's opposable thumbs and big toes enable it to grasp branches well. It climbs slowly and catches prey with both hands. Slender lorises can run but cannot swim. They mainly consume insects, but also eat plant shoots, young leaves, some fruits, birds' eggs, and small vertebrates. Females may give birth twice a year, usu-ally to one or two young at a time.

The **potto** (*Perodicticus potto*) lives in the tropical forests of west-central Africa, sleeping in trees during the day. It has thick, woolly fur, which may be brownish gray or a dark reddish brown, and a bushy tail. Its hands and feet are designed for grasping, and the second toe of each foot has a long, sharp claw. Pottos, which are about a foot long, climb slowly and do not leap from branch to branch. The potto's main food is fruit, but it also eats tree gums and insects, licking up ants, and sometimes eats small birds and bats. A female-male pair will remain together all year, but only during their night activity; pottos sleep alone during the day. It is very rare for more than one potto to be born at a time. Pottos have been known to live for more than twenty years.

The **southern flying squirrel** (*Glaucomys volans*) actually glides, rather than flying. It is found in the eastern United States, from Canada to Florida and the Gulf of Mexico, but is rarely seen. These squirrels and their northern relatives are the only nocturnal squirrels. Their thick, soft, glossy fur is olive-brown on the upper body and white below. A folded layer of loose skin on each side of the body, from front leg to hind leg, enables them to glide downward from one tree to another. These squirrels live in forests and nest in hollow trees. They eat seeds, nuts, fruit, insects, and birds' eggs. Two to six young are born at a time, twice a year.

The **raccoon** *(Procyon lotor)* is found in most parts of the United States, in southern Canada, and in Mexico and Central America. Its body hair is a pepper-and-salt mixture of black and white. Its distinctive features are the black "mask" on its face and the yellowish-white rings on its bushy tail (sometimes the rings are not very distinct). Raccoons like to live by streams or lakes, in or near wooded areas or rocky cliffs. They usually make their dens in hollow trees. Their varied diet includes seeds, berries, nuts, grain, insects, shellfish, frogs, and birds' eggs, and they will raid people's garbage. They have five clawed toes on each foot, and manipulate items well with their hands, as monkeys do. They are good climbers and swimmers.

The **kinkajou** *(Potos flavus)* lives in forest trees from southern Mexico to central Brazil. The hair on the upper parts of its body is tawny olive, tawny yellow, or brown. On the lower parts it is tawny yellow, buff, or brownish yellow. The kinkajou has a long, prehensile tail, which it wraps around branches, and a narrow, long tongue. Its hind legs are longer than its front legs, and it has short, sharp claws on its toes. It sleeps in a hollow tree during the day, and at night forages for fruit, honey, insects, and small animals. Kinkajous move around alone or in pairs. They have been known to live more than twenty years. Usually only one is born at a time, but occasionally two are born together.

The **aye-aye** *(Daubentonia madagascariensis)* evolved only on the large island of Madagascar, off the east coast of Africa. The species has teetered on the brink of extinction repeatedly during this century. Aye-ayes have coarse, straight, dark hair; most of the face and throat are yellowish white. Their eyes and ears are large. The long, narrow third finger on each hand is used for grooming and for extracting food from hard-to-reach places. Aye-ayes live in forests, mangrove swamps, and bamboo thickets, but most of their habitat has been destroyed. In the daytime they sleep in elaborate nests that they construct from leaves and twigs. They mainly eat fruit and insect larvae. Aye-ayes reproduce less than once a year, and only one is born at a time.

33

The **long-eared owl** *(Asio otus)* lives in woodlands in the south-central and southwestern United States, and in Canada, as well as in the Middle East and North Africa. It is 13 to 16 inches tall, and slender. Distinctive long tufts of feathers adorn its ears, which are close together. Like other owls, it has excellent vision and hearing and can turn its head almost in a full circle. Its face is rust colored, and it has many streaks and bars of brown and black on its breast and belly. During the day it often roosts motionless, sometimes in groups, close to the trunk of a tree with thick foliage. By night these owls hunt over open fields and marshes. They usually are silent, except in mating season, when their call is a long "hooooo."

The **serval** *(Felis serval)* lives in Morocco and Algeria in North Africa, and in much of Africa south of the Sahara Desert. Its legs and its neck are long, and it has very large ears. The fur on the upper parts of its body varies from off-white to dark gold; on the lower parts it is paler, even white. All of the fur has small dark spots, or sometimes large dark spots that blend into stripes on the head and back. The serval's tail has several dark rings and a black tip. Servals tend to live near streams, in dense vegetation. They mainly eat rodents, but also leap up to capture roosting birds. Females may give birth twice a year, usually producing one to four young. Hunted for their skins and also killed by farmers, servals have been endangered for many years in some areas.

The **fennec fox** *(Fennecus zerda),* which lives in the Sahara Desert and on the Arabian Peninsula, can survive for long periods without water. It is the smallest fox, but has very big ears for its size. It is the palest-colored fox, with its upper body parts reddish cream, light fawn, or almost white, and the lower parts white. The tail has a black tip. The fur is long and thick. Fennec foxes can run well in loose sand because they have hair on the soles of their feet. They are very fast diggers, and live in long burrows under the sand. They can jump far upward and forward. Their diet includes plant material, small rodents, birds and their eggs, lizards, and insects. Both females and males defend newborn young; two to five are born at a time.

The **boa constrictor** (*Boa constrictor*) is found from northern Mexico to Argentina in South America, and on some islands in the Caribbean Sea. It lives in various habitats, from dense rain forests to arid areas at the edges of deserts. It is very unusual to find one of these snakes that is more than 15 feet long. Boa constrictors spend much more time in trees than do their larger relatives, anacondas, and they spend much less time in water. They mainly eat large lizards and birds, but sometimes kill larger animals by encircling them in their coils and pressing so tightly that they cannot breathe, as the anaconda and other boas do. Boas have very powerful digestive juices. Newborn snakes average about 20 inches in length; 20 to 60 of them are born at a time.

The **ruffed lemur** *(Varecia variegata)* is the largest member of the Lemuridae family, commonly known as lemurs. It lives in the narrow remaining strip of rain forest on the eastern coast of the large island of Madagascar, off the east coast of Africa. Lemurs evolved only on Madagascar, where no true monkeys developed. The ruffed lemur has long, soft hair, and its ears are hidden by a ruff of hair. There are two subspecies, both with variegated coloring. One is black and white, while the other is mostly reddish in color, with black and white markings. Ruffed lemurs are most active in the early evening and soon after nightfall. They are endangered because of destruction of their forest habitat and because they have been hunted for export sales.

The **sugarglider possum** (*Petaurus breviceps*) lives in northern and eastern Australia, on the large island of New Guinea to the north, and on some small islands nearby. Its fine, silky fur usually is grayish on the upper parts of the body and paler below. Sugargliders resemble flying squirrels in form (see page 30), but their tails are furry. These active creatures can glide long distances and can catch moths in flight by leaping. During the day, they sleep—sometimes in groups—in nests made of leaves placed inside a hollow part of a tree. They feed on tree sap, flowers, nectar, insects, spiders, and small animals.

The **short-tail shrew** (*Blarina brevicanda*) lives in forests, grasslands, marshes, and brushy areas throughout the eastern United States and in southeastern Canada. It is active both by day and by night. It has a head and body length of three to four inches, very small eyes, and no external ears. These shrews tunnel through the earth and through the snow, and also use tunnels made by other creatures. They make nests beneath logs, stumps, rocks, or debris. Their diet includes insects, worms, and snails. Newborns (usually five to eight are born at a time) are about the size of a honeybee, hairless, and pink-skinned.

The **cavy** or **guinea pig** *(Cavia guianae)* is one of six wild species of rodent, found in many parts of South America, that are related to the guinea pig popular as a pet in North America and Europe, which was domesticated in South America as a source of food long before Europeans arrived there. The wild species have long, coarse hair that is not uniform in color, but looks gray or brown overall. They have short legs and ears, and no visible tail. Cavies are found in open grasslands, at the edges of forests, in swamps, and in rocky areas. They live in burrows or in thick vegetation, feeding mostly at twilight and in the evening hours. They are vegetarians.

The **coyote** *(Canis latrans)* is found from Alaska and Canada to the southern edge of Central America. It stays in a burrow or den during the day and begins hunting at twilight. It has long fur and a bushy tail, with a buff-gray coloration above and a paler color below. Coyotes, among the fastest-running animals in North America, can achieve speeds of about 40 miles (64 km) per hour. Their main diet is jackrabbits and rodents, but they also hunt deer. A coyote sometimes will hunt with a badger and share the burrowing rodents they catch. A female-male pair of coyotes may live and hunt together for years. Coyotes use many sounds to communicate, including the howl for which they are best known. An average of six coyotes are born at a time.

The **tawny frogmouth** *(Podargus strigoides)*, which may be reddish brown or grayish, is found in forested areas of Australia and on the island of Tasmania south of that continent. Other frogmouths are native to Southeast Asia's peninsulas and islands. Its eyes are said to be owl-like. This bird's common name indicates that people think its wide-opening mouth looks like a frog's mouth. The bird feels flying insects with the whisker-like feathers around its mouth. The tawny frogmouth is about 20 inches long. It captures large insects, small lizards, and mice by hunting at night, among tree branches and on the ground. Its call sounds like "more-pork" or "mopoke." Females hatch two or three eggs at a time.

The **caracal** (*Caracal caracal*), a wild cat found on the Arabian Peninsula, as far east as northwestern India, and in most of Africa, is recognizable by its long, narrow, upright, pointed ears, which are black on the outside and have tufts of black hair at the tips. The animal has reddish-brown body fur, with white fur on the chin, throat, and belly. Caracals live in dry country—wooded, savannah, or scrub—but avoid deserts. They run fast and climb and jump well, capturing birds, rodents, and small antelope by chasing and leaping. From one to six kittens are born at a time. Caracals have become rare in some areas as a result of being hunted by people because they sometimes kill poultry.